# Murray

### by Iain Gray

**PUBLISHING**

WRITING *to* REMEMBER

79 Main Street, Newtongrange,
Midlothian EH22 4NA
Tel: 0131 344 0414
E-mail: info@lang-syne.co.uk
www.langsyneshop.co.uk

Design by Dorothy Meikle
Printed by Printwell Ltd
© Lang Syne Publishers Ltd 2023

All rights reserved. No part of this publication may be reproduced, stored or introduced into a retrieval system, or transmitted in any form or by any means (electronic, mechanical, photocopying, recording or otherwise) without the prior written permission of Lang Syne Publishers Ltd.

ISBN 978-1-85217-594-8

# Murray

**MOTTO:**
Furth fortune and fill the fetters
(and)
Quite ready.

**CREST:**
A demi-savage wreathed about the waist
and temples with laurel and holding
a dagger in one hand and a key in the other
(and)
A mermaid holding a mirror
in one hand and a comb in the other.

**NAME** variations include:
Moray
Morey
Morrey
Murrey
Murry

## Chapter one:

# The origins of popular surnames

by George Forbes and Iain Gray

***If you don't know where you came from, you won't know where you're going*** **is a frequently quoted observation and one that has a particular resonance today when there has been a marked upsurge in interest in genealogy, with increasing numbers of people curious to trace their family roots.**

Main sources for genealogical research include census returns and official records of births, marriages and deaths – and the key to unlocking the detail they contain is obviously a family surname, one that has been 'inherited' and passed from generation to generation.

No matter our station in life, we all have a surname – but it was not until about the middle of the fourteenth century that the practice of being identified by a particular surname became commonly established throughout the British Isles.

Previous to this, it was normal for a person to be identified through the use of only a forename.

But as population gradually increased and there were many more people with the same forename, surnames were adopted to distinguish one person, or community, from another.

Many common English surnames are patronymic in origin, meaning they stem from the forename of one's father – with 'Johnson,' for example, indicating 'son of John.'

It was the Normans, in the wake of their eleventh century conquest of Anglo-Saxon England, a pivotal moment in the nation's history, who first brought surnames into usage – although it was a gradual process.

For the Normans, these were names initially based on the title of their estates, local villages and chateaux in France to distinguish and identify these landholdings.

Such grand descriptions also helped enhance the prestige of these warlords and generally glorify their lofty positions high above the humble serfs slaving away below in the pecking order who had only single names, often with Biblical connotations as in Pierre and Jacques.

The only descriptive distinctions among the peasantry concerned their occupations, like 'Pierre the swineherd' or 'Jacques the ferryman.'

Roots of surnames that came into usage in England not only included Norman-French, but also Old French, Old Norse, Old English, Middle English, German, Latin, Greek, Hebrew and the Gaelic languages of the Celts.

The Normans themselves were originally Vikings, or 'Northmen', who raided, colonised and eventually settled down around the French coastline.

They had sailed up the Seine in their longboats in 900AD under their ferocious leader Rollo and ruled the roost in north eastern France before sailing over to conquer England in 1066 under Duke William of Normandy – better known to posterity as William the Conqueror, or King William I of England.

Granted lands in the newly-conquered England, some of their descendants later acquired territories in Wales, Scotland and Ireland – taking not only their own surnames, but also the practice of adopting a surname, with them.

But it was in England where Norman rule and custom first impacted, particularly in relation to the adoption of surnames.

This is reflected in the famous *Domesday Book*, a massive survey of much of England and Wales, ordered by William I, to determine who owned what, what it was worth and therefore how much they were liable to pay in taxes to the voracious Royal Exchequer.

Completed in 1086 and now held in the National Archives in Kew, London, 'Domesday' was an Old English word meaning 'Day of Judgement.'

This was because, in the words of one contemporary chronicler, "its decisions, like those of the Last Judgement, are unalterable."

It had been a requirement of all those English landholders – from the richest to the poorest – that they identify themselves for the purposes of the survey and for future reference by means of a surname.

This is why the *Domesday Book*, although written in Latin as was the practice for several centuries with both civic and ecclesiastical records, is an invaluable source for the early appearance of a wide range of English surnames.

Several of these names were coined in connection with occupations.

These include Baker and Smith, while Cooks, Chamberlains, Constables and Porters were to be found carrying out duties in large medieval households.

The church's influence can be found in names such as Bishop, Friar and Monk while the popular name of Bennett derives from the late fifth to mid-sixth century Saint Benedict, founder of the Benedictine order of monks.

The early medical profession is represented by Barber, while businessmen produced names that include Merchant and Sellers.

Down at the village watermill, the names that cropped up included Millar/Miller, Walker and Fuller, while other self-explanatory trades included Cooper, Tailor, Mason and Wright.

Even the scenery was utilised as in Moor, Hill, Wood and Forrest – while the hunt and the chase supplied names that include Hunter, Falconer, Fowler and Fox.

Colours are also a source of popular surnames, as in Black, Brown, Gray/Grey, Green and White, and would have denoted the colour of the clothing the person habitually wore or, apart from the obvious exception of 'Green', one's hair colouring or even complexion.

The surname Red developed into Reid, while

Blue was rare and no-one wanted to be associated with yellow.

Rather self-important individuals took surnames that include Goodman and Wiseman, while physical attributes crept into surnames such as Small and Little.

Many families proudly boast the heraldic device known as a Coat of Arms, as featured on our front cover.

The central motif of the Coat of Arms would originally have been what was borne on the shield of a warrior to distinguish himself from others on the battlefield.

Not featured on the Coat of Arms, but highlighted on page three, is the family motto and related crest – with the latter frequently different from the central motif.

Adding further variety to the rich cultural heritage that is represented by surnames is the appearance in recent times in lists of the 100 most common names found in England of ones that include Khan, Patel and Singh – names that have proud roots in the vast sub-continent of India.

Echoes of a far distant past can still be found in our surnames and they can be borne with pride in commemoration of our forebears.

*Chapter two:*

# Ancient roots

**Ranked at 98th in some lists of the 100 most common surnames found in England today, 'Murray' has roots that stretch back to not only the ancient Picts of Scotland but also to a warrior knight who was involved in one of the most pivotal events in the frequently turbulent history of the British Isles.**

To untangle the complex genealogical skein that proud bearers of the Murray name are heirs to and to explain why bearers of the name today are not identified with any particular part of England, we have to travel back through the dim mists of time to 1066.

By this date, England had become a nation with several powerful competitors to the throne.

In what were extremely complex family, political and military machinations, the monarch was Harold II, who had succeeded to the throne following the death of Edward the Confessor.

But his right to the throne was contested by two powerful competitors – his brother-in-law

King Harold Hardrada of Norway, in alliance with Tostig, Harold II's brother, and Duke William II of Normandy.

In what has become known as The Year of Three Battles, Hardrada invaded England and gained victory over the English king on September 20 at the battle of Fulford, in Yorkshire.

Five days later, however, Harold II decisively defeated his brother-in-law and brother at the battle of Stamford Bridge.

But he had little time to celebrate his victory, having to immediately march south from Yorkshire to encounter a mighty invasion force led by Duke William that had landed at Hastings, in East Sussex.

Harold's battle-hardened but exhausted force of Anglo-Saxon soldiers confronted the Normans on October 14 in a battle subsequently depicted on the Bayeux tapestry – a 23ft. long strip of embroidered linen thought to have been commissioned eleven years after the event by the Norman Odo of Bayeux.

Harold drew up a strong defensive position, at the top of Senlac Hill, building a shield wall to repel Duke William's cavalry and infantry.

The Normans suffered heavy losses, but through a combination of the deadly skill of their archers and the ferocious determination of their cavalry they eventually won the day.

Anglo-Saxon morale had collapsed on the battlefield as word spread through the ranks that Harold had been killed.

William was declared King of England on December 25, and the complete subjugation of his Anglo-Saxon subjects followed.

Those Normans and others who had fought on his behalf were rewarded with the lands of Anglo-Saxons, and within an astonishingly short space of time Norman manners, customs and law were imposed on England – laying the basis for what subsequently became established 'English' custom and practice.

Among those who helped William and his successors to consolidate Norman power in the aftermath of the Conquest was a Flemish warlord known as Freskin.

It was during the reign from 1124 to 1153 of Scotland's David I, who had spent some time at the Norman court in London and had become enamoured with the Normans and their followers, that he granted lands in his own realm to nobles and warlords such as Freskin – in order to quell disorder in some parts of his often unruly kingdom.

Freskin was given lands in what is now modern-day West Lothian and also granted what had been the ancient Pictish kingdom of Moray, in north-eastern Scotland, and known in Gaelic as *Moireabh*.

Freskin and his sons consolidated their grip on Moray through intermarriage with what had been the distinguished Royal House of Moray and took the surname 'de Moravia' – 'of Moray' – which later became 'Murray.'

The Chiefs of present-day Clan Murray, whose titles include Duke of Atholl and Earl of Tullibardine, descend from William de Moravia, a younger grandson of Freskin, while the Chiefs of Clan Sutherland descend from Hugh de Moravia, his eldest grandson.

Any present day bearers of the Murray name who are not necessarily Scottish by birth but may be able to trace a descent from William de Moravia and his lineage, are meanwhile entitled to share in Clan Murray's proud heritage.

The Murrays came to figure prominently in the historical record.

One bearer of the name with a rather unusual claim to historical fame was William Murray, who was the 'whipping boy' of Charles I.

Born in about 1600 in Dysart, Fifeshire, the son of a Scottish minister, William Murray, a descendant of the Murrays of Tullibardine, it was as a young lad that he was officially chosen as companion to Charles, then Prince Charles.

It was in the role of 'whipping boy', considered then an honour and only given to highly-born young men like Murray, that he would be punished – for example by whipping – as a 'substitute' for the prince when he misbehaved.

In keeping with the belief of the 'divine right of kings', that existed from about the 15th century until the fall of the Stuart dynasty in the late seventeenth century, only the king himself was able to chastise his son.

With the monarch too frequently engaged with other high matters of state to find the time to punish his son for misdemeanours, the solution was to substitute a 'whipping boy' to take the punishment on his son's behalf.

William Murray and the young prince became close friends and it was in recognition of their intimate bond that when the prince ascended the throne as Charles I he chose him as one of his highly trusted advisers and, in 1643, created him Earl of Dysart.

This was during the English Civil War, when Charles had incurred the wrath of Parliament by his insistence on the divine right of monarchs, and added to this was fear of Catholic 'subversion' against the state and the king's stubborn refusal to grant demands for religious and constitutional concessions.

Matters came to a head with the outbreak of the war in 1642, with Parliamentary forces, known as the New Model Army and commanded by Oliver Cromwell and Sir Thomas Fairfax, arrayed against the Royalist army of the king.

In what became an increasingly bloody and complex conflict, spreading to Scotland and Ireland and with rapidly shifting loyalties on both sides, the king was eventually captured and executed in January of 1649 on the orders of Parliament.

William Murray, faithful childhood friend and later adviser to the ill-fated Charles I, died in exile in France in 1655.

*Chapter three:*

# Honours and distinction

**In keeping with the close association that the Murrays have had with royalty, Lady Augusta Murray, born in London in 1768 and the daughter of John Murray, 4th Earl of Dunmore, and Lady Charlotte Stewart, daughter of the 6th Earl of Galloway, had a particularly tragic romance.**

It was in April of 1793 that she secretly married Prince Augustus Frederick, the sixth son of George III, in a ceremony in Rome – not revealing their true identities.

The couple underwent another 'secret' marriage ceremony in London a few months later – but once the truth came out both marriage ceremonies were deemed in contravention of the Royal Marriages Act of 1772 and the marriage annulled.

But the couple lived together until 1801, when dynastic pressures on the prince cruelly forced him to leave the lady who was the love of his life.

Lady Augusta died in 1830, while the prince, by this time having been created Duke of Sussex, later married Lady Cecilia Underwood.

Anne Murray, born Anne Home-Drummond in Edinburgh in 1814, was the courtier and close friend and confidant of Queen Victoria who, after her marriage to George Murray, 2nd Baron Glenlyon and 6th Duke of Atholl, became Duchess of Atholl; she died in 1897.

Bearers of the Murray name have also gained distinction through their actions on the bloody field of battle, with a number having been awarded the Victoria Cross (VC), the highest award for gallantry in the face of enemy action for British and Commonwealth forces.

Born in Cork City in 1859, James Murray was an Irish recipient of the honour during the First Boer War of 1880 to 1881.

He had been a lance-corporal in the 2nd Battalion, The Connaught Rangers, when in January of 1881 at Elandsfontein, near Pretoria in South Africa, he braved heavy enemy fire to rescue a wounded comrade.

He died in 1942, while his VC is now on display at the National Army Museum, Chelsea.

Born in Tasmania in 1880, Henry Murray, better known as Harry Murray, was an Australian recipient of the honour during the carnage of the First

World War. Recognised as the most highly decorated soldier of the conflict, it was in February of 1917, during the battle of the Somme, that as a lieutenant-colonel he commanded a company that led a daring and successful attack against an enemy position.

Previous to this, he had been awarded the Distinguished Conduct Medal for his actions during the Gallipoli Campaign, while he was also awarded the Distinguished Service Medal shortly before his actions at the battle of the Somme; he died in 1966.

Also during the First World War, General Sir Archibald James Murray, born in 1860, was the distinguished military officer who served for a short period after the outbreak of the conflict in August of 1914 as Chief of Staff to the British Expeditionary Force (BEF); he died in 1945.

From the battlefield to the world of publishing, John Murray was the founder of the company that bears his name to this day.

Born in Edinburgh in 1745 he founded the John Murray publishing house in London in 1768 and also published the influential the *English Review* in addition to being a founder of the former London evening newspaper *The Star*.

He died in 1793, while it was under his son John Murray II that the John Murray publishing house flourished even more.

Famous authors published from their premises in Albemarle Street, in Mayfair, include Sir Walter Scott, Jane Austin, Washington Irving and the poet Lord Byron – most notably concerning the latter's 1812 *Childe Harold's Pilgrimage*.

This became an instant best-seller, with the first print run selling out within five days, and Byron later remarking: "I awoke one morning and found myself famous."

In 1824, following Byron's death, John Murray II entered the annals of literary infamy when, along with five of the poet's other friends and executors, he consigned the manuscript to the flames of his fireplace.

This was done because of fears that some of the scandalous details revealed in the often dissolute poet's memoirs would have damaged his reputation to posterity.

Under John Murray III, born in 1808 and who died in 1892, the John Murray publishing house published seminal works that include, in 1859, Charles Darwin's *Origin of Species*, while also launching

*Murray Handbooks* – recognised as the precursors of modern-day travel guides.

The John Murray imprint was acquired by Hodder Headline in 2002 and, two years later, by the French Lagardère Group and it now exists as a valued imprint of the Lagardère brand Hatchette UK.

In 2005, the archive of John Murray Publishers from 1768 to 1920 and including the original manuscript of *Origin of Species*, was purchased by the National Library of Scotland for £31.2m with help from the Heritage Lottery Fund, the Scottish Executive and through a number of fund-raising initiatives.

In the world of politics, Lionel Murray, better known as Len Murray, was the British Labour politician who served from 1973 until 1984 as General Secretary of the Trades Union Congress (TUC).

Born in 1922 near Telford, Shropshire, the son of a farmworker, he died in 2004 after having been elevated to the Peerage of the United Kingdom as Baron Murray of Epping Forest.

In contemporary politics, Dr Elaine Murray, born in 1954 in Hitchin, Hertfordshire is the Labour politician who has served since 1999 as Member of the Scottish Parliament (MSP) for Dumfriesshire.

Born to Scottish parents and the recipient of a doctorate in physical chemistry, she has served as Shadow Minister for the Environment in the Scottish Parliament.

In the competitive world of business, David Andrew Murray, better known as David Murray and more formally as Sir David Andrew Murray, is the Scottish entrepreneur who is a former owner and chairman of Rangers Football Club.

Born in Ayr in 1951, he was aged 23 by the time he formed his company Murray International Metals and, by 2008, his personal wealth was estimated at £720m.

He bought Rangers in 1988 for £6m, stepping down as its chairman in 2009. During his tenure the club won 26 Cups and 15 League Championships.

In 1976, nearly two years after having formed his company – which now has interests that include not only the distribution of structural steel but also surface mining and commercial property development – he lost both legs in a car crash when returning from a rugby match.

It was as a supporter of fellow amputees that in 1996 he established the Murray Foundation, while he was knighted in 2007 for services to business in Scotland.

Bearers of the Murray name have also stamped their mark on the pages of the historical record of medicine.

Born in 1919 in Milford, Massachusetts, Joseph Edward Murray was the plastic surgeon who, in December of 1954, performed the first successful human kidney transplant.

This was on the identical twins Richard and Ronald Herrick, assisted by other physicians and surgeons, at the then Peter Bent Brigham Hospital in Boston.

A graduate of Harvard Medical School and, during the Second World War, a pioneer of plastic surgery techniques on wounded and disfigured soldiers, he shared the Nobel Prize in Physiology or Medicine with E. Donnall Thomas for their discoveries concerning organ and cell transplantation in the treatment of human disease.

The recipient of a number of honours and awards that include the American Surgical Association's Medal for Distinguished Service to Surgery, he died in 2012.

One particularly inventive bearer of the

proud name of Murray was Thomas E. Murray, who developed electric power plants for New York City in addition to inventing the electric safety fuse and the dimmer switch.

Born in 1860 in Albany, New York and the holder of 462 U.S. patents and the recipient of honours that include induction into the National Inventor's Hall of Fame, he died in 1929.

*Chapter four:*

# On the world stage

**One of an American acting dynasty, William James Murray, better known as Bill Murray, is the actor and comedian born in 1950 in the Chicago suburb of Wilmette.**

Of Irish-American roots, the son of a timber salesman and one of eight brothers and sisters, he is best known for films that include the 1979 *Meatballs*, the 1980 *Caddyshack*, the 1984 *Ghostbusters* and, from 1993, *Groundhog Day*.

Other film credits include the 2001 *The Royal Tenenbaums* and the 2003 *Lost in Translation* – which earned him an Academy Award nomination for Best Actor.

Also one of the stars from 1977 to 1980 of the American television comedy show *Saturday Night Live*, for which he won an Emmy Award, he was first introduced to the comedy circuit by his older brother Brian Murray, better known as **Brian Doyle-Murray**.

Born in 1945, the comedian, screenwriter and actor has appeared with his brother Bill in films that include *Caddyshack* and *Groundhog Day*.

His other brothers, **John Murray**, born in 1958, is the actor whose screen credits include the 1988 *Scrooged* – along with brothers Bill and Brian – while **Joel Murray**, born in 1963, is best known for his roles in television series that include *Mad Men*, while he also appeared on the big screen in films that include the 2011 *God Bless America*.

On British shores, **Barbara Ann Murray** was the actress whose television credits include *Danger Man*, *The Saint* and *Department S*, while film credits include the 1949 *Passport to Pimlico*, the 1957 *Campbell's Kingdom* and, from 1980, *The Curse of King Tut's Tomb*; born in 1929, she died in 2014.

Best known for his roles on British television dramas and soaps that include *The Bill* and *EastEnders*, **Billy Murray**, born in 1941 in the east end of London, is the actor whose big screen credits include the 2006 *Rollin' with the Nines* and the 2009 *Doghouse*, while he is also one of the 'voices' on the *Call of Duty* series of video games.

Known for her role of Suzie Birchall in the British television soap *Coronation Street*, **Cheryl Murray**, born in Liverpool in 1952, is the actress whose other television credits include the comedy *Hi-de-Hi!*

Born in 1919 in Greenock, Inverclyde, Charles Thomas McKinnon Murray was the Scottish comedian and actor noted for his droll and quirky sense of humour and better known as **Chic Murray**.

It was while working as an apprentice in an Inverclyde shipyard that he also took to the stage as a musician in a number of amateur productions, until he met his future wife Maidie Dickson, who was already an established star on the entertainment circuit.

Forming a double act, the 6ft. 3in. Murray and the 4ft. 11in. Maidie were billed as "The Tall Droll and the Small Doll" and, later, as Maidie and Murray.

Later forging a successful solo act, in the early 1970s Murray was the star of the BBC Scotland television series *Chic's Chat* – sporting his trademark flat cap better known in Scotland as a 'bunnet.'

Also with film credits that include the 1967 *Casino Royale*, the 1981 *Gregory's Girl* and, from 1983, *Saigon: Year of the Cat*, on the stage he gained acclaim for his role of former Liverpool Football Club manager and fellow Scot Bill Shankly in *You'll Never Walk Alone*.

He died in 1985, while in 2005 he was placed at 38th out of 50 in The Comedian's Comedian – a poll in which comedians chose their own particular favourite or influential comedy act of all time.

A descendant through his father, Lieutenant Ingram Hay Murray, of John Murray, 3rd Duke of Atholl and, through his mother, of the writer William Makepeace Thackeray, author of *Vanity Fair*, Alastair James Hay Murray is the English comedian better known as **Al Murray**.

Born in 1968 in Stewkley, Buckinghamshire, and best known for his television series *The Pub Landlord*, as a stand-up comedian he won the Perrier Award for Comedy at the 1999 Edinburgh Festival Fringe, while in 2007 he was voted 16th greatest stand-up comic in Channel 4's 100 Greatest Stand-Ups.

Best known for her role of Cassie Ainsworth in the television drama series *Skins* and of Gilly in the series *Game of Thrones*, **Hannah Murray** is the English actress born Tegan Lauren Hannah Murray in Bristol in 1989.

Born in 1921, **Gordon Murray** is the British puppeteer and television producer famed as the creator of highly popular children's programmes that include *Trumpton*, *Camberwick Green* and *Chigley*, while in the world of broadcasting **Jenni Murray**, nee

Bailey, is the journalist and broadcaster best known as a presenter of BBC Radio 4's *Woman's Hour*.

Born in 1950 in Barnsley, Yorkshire, she was appointed a Dame Commander of the Order of the British Empire (DBE) in 2011 for her services to broadcasting, eleven years after being honoured with an OBE.

Bearers of the Murray name have also excelled in the highly competitive world of sport – not least on the tennis court.

Born in Glasgow in 1987 but spending most of his young life in Dunblane, north of Stirling, Andrew Barron Murray is the Scottish tennis star better known as **Andy Murray**.

Winner in 2013 of the Wimbledon men's singles championship title and in 2012 of the Olympic men's singles title, his many other wins include the U.S. Open in 2012.

The recipient of an OBE and voted BBC Sports Personality of the Year in 2013, the Grand Slam singles champion has attained success on the tennis court despite being born with a physical disability known as a bipartite patella – involving problems with the fusing of the bones in the kneecap.

As a child, he was present as a pupil in

Dunblane Primary School in 1996 when a deranged local man, Thomas Hamilton, shot and killed sixteen pupils and a teacher.

His older brother **Jamie Murray**, born in 1986, is the tennis player who specialises in doubles and who, in 2007, won the mixed doubles title at Wimbledon with Jelena Janković.

Coach for a time for both her sons Andy and Jamie, Judith Murray, née Erskine, and better known as **Judy Murray**, was born in 1959 in Bridge of Allan.

The daughter of Roy Erskine, a Scottish former footballer who played in the 1950s for Stirling Albion, the former badminton and tennis player was appointed captain of the British Fed Cup team in 2011.

From the tennis court to the golf course, **Andrew Murray**, born in Manchester in 1956, is the English professional golfer who played from 1979 to 1995 on the European Tour while, in the boxing ring, his namesake **Andrew Murray**, born in 1982 in Cavan, is the boxer who took the Irish light welterweight title in 2007.

On the athletics track, **Yvonne Murray**, born in 1964 in Musselburgh, East Lothian, and now also known by her married name of Yvonne Murray-Mooney, is the Scottish former long-distance, road-running and middle-distance athlete whose many accolades include winning a bronze medal in the 300-metres event at the 1988 Olympics and gold in the 10,000-metres event at the 1994 Commonwealth Games.

The recipient of an MBE, she is also an inductee of the Scottish Sports Hall of Fame.

Also born in Musselburgh, in his case in 1976, **Scott Murray** is the Scottish rugby union player who, in addition to playing for clubs that include Saracens and French club Castres, holds 87 caps for having played for his national team.

Back to the athletics track, **Samantha Murray**, born in 1989 in Preston, Lancashire is the English modern pentathlete who won the silver medal in the event at the 2012 London Olympics and, in the same year, a bronze at the World Championships.

One particularly intrepid bearer of the Murray name – and one who has displayed an impressive amount of physical stamina – is **Andrew Murray**, the Scottish medical doctor whose many achievements include completing a near 2,700 mile 'run' in 2011 from John o' Groats, in the far north of Scotland, through to the Sahara Desert.

Born in 1980 and also the holder of many

other endurance race titles that include running up Britain's highest peaks in a single day, in 2012 he was appointed to the Scottish Government as 'physical activity champion.'

In the world of music, Morna Anne Murray, better known as **Anne Murray**, is the best-selling Canadian singer whose many hits include her 1970 *Snowbird*.

Born in 1945 in Springhill, Nova Scotia and the recipient of honours and awards that include induction into the Canadian Country Music Hall of Fame and a star on the Hollywood Walk of Fame, her other hits include the 1978 *You Needed Me* and, from 1984, *Just Another Woman in Love*.

In a much different musical genre, **David Murray**, born in 1956 in Edmonton, London is the guitarist and songwriter who is a member of the British heavy metal band Iron Maiden.

The recipient of the Gold Badge of Merit from the British Academy of Songwriters, Composers and Authors, Lionel Michael Stitcher is the English songwriter and record producer better known as **Mitch Murray**.

Born in 1940 in Hove, Sussex, he is the recipient of two Ivor Novello Awards for songs he composed, or co-composed. These include the Gerry and the Pacemakers hit *How Do You Do It?*, the Freddie and the Dreamers hit *I'm Telling You Now*, Tony Christie's *I Did What I Did For Maria* and, recorded by Georgie Fame, *The Ballad of Bonnie and Clyde*.

One of the first presenters of the BBC weekly television show *Top of the Pops* when it began in 1964, Peter Murray James is the radio and television presenter better known as **Pete Murray**.

Born in 1925 and beginning his broadcasting career with Radio Luxembourg in 1949 and later working for the BBC, he was voted BBC Radio Personality of the Year in 1973 and 1976 and is also the recipient of an OBE.

One of the most popular musical entertainers of the 1950s, Ruby Florence Murray was the Irish singer born in Belfast in 1935 and better known as **Ruby Murray**.

With top-selling hits that include her 1954 *Heartbeat* and the 1955 *Softly, Softly* she died in 1996, while one of her rather more unusual claims to fame is that 'Ruby Murray' has now entered the lexicon as rhyming slang for the popular spicy foodstuff 'curry.'